GU00792977

The Vikings

written and
illustrated by

Alaric Birkett

 Hulton Educational

Acknowledgements

First published in Great Britain 1985
by Hulton Educational Publications Ltd
Raans Rd, Amersham, Bucks HP6 6JJ

© Alaric Birkett 1985
Edited and designed by Susan Baker

ISBN 0 7175 1321 1

Typeset by CG Graphic Services, Aylesbury, Bucks
Printed in Hong Kong

Contents

1 The Fury of
the Northmen

The Anglo-Saxon Chronicle mentions that, in A.D.789, three ship's crews landed on the Dorset coast of England:

> Hearing of this, the local sheriff, who lived at Dorchester, leapt on his horse with a small group of followers and rode to the port, believing them to be peaceful traders rather than pirates; and rudely ordered them to be taken to the King. But the sheriff and his men were killed immediately.

Four years later more ships were seen off the coast of Northumbria. They were long and narrow with high prows and large, square sails. The monk, Simeon of Durham, vividly describes what then happened:

> They spread out on all sides like ravenous wolves, robbing, tearing and slaughtering, not only beasts of burden, sheep and cattle, but even priests and deacons, and communities of monks and nuns. And they came to the church on Lindisfarne and laid everything waste. They plundered and trampled on the holy places with filthy feet, dug up the altars and seized all the treasures of the holy

Church. They murdered some of the monks and carried away others in chains. Some they drove out, naked and loaded with insults, the rest they drowned in the sea.

These were the first recorded raids of the Vikings. For the next 250 years these fierce men from the North were to raid the shores of Western Europe. Terror filled the heart of the ploughman as he turned from his work and saw, rounding a bend in the river, the terrible dragon's head, the huge, striped sail and the grim, mail-clad warriors who struck the water in regular time with their oars as they made for the bank. Congregations huddled together in their churches as priests called out to God:

From the fury of the Northmen, O Lord, deliver us!

At first, the Vikings simply made quick raids on small farms and villages. Later, as their confidence grew, they came back in larger numbers, destroying cities and conquering whole countries. Finally, they settled down to farm their new lands.

The Vikings were more than just fierce warriors. They were great and fearless sailors as well. Their beautifully designed longships took them across seas where no man had dared venture before: to places as far west as Greenland, and even America; across the Baltic, and through Europe along the great rivers.

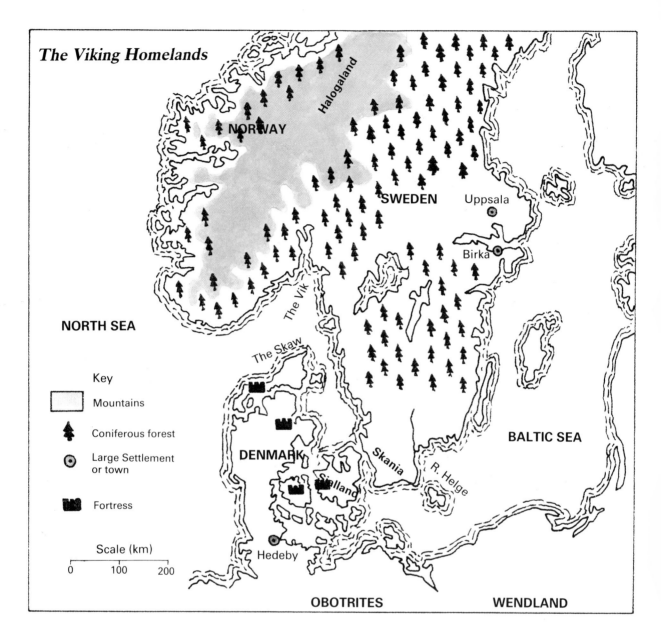

The Viking Homelands

Key

Mountains

Coniferous forest

Large Settlement or town

Fortress

Scale (km)

0   100   200

The Viking Homelands

The Vikings came from **Scandinavia**, that is the lands now known as **Denmark**, **Norway** and **Sweden**. These countries were described by a German called Adam of Bremen who lived around A.D.1075. He said:

Denmark consists almost entirely of islands. The barren soil is hardly farmed at all, and large towns only exist where fjords (deep inlets) cut into the land.

Norway is the harshest of all countries because of its rugged mountains and extreme cold. . . . Forced by the poverty of their homeland (the Norwegians) venture abroad to bring back from their raids the goods which other countries so plentifully produce.

But much of Sweden is fertile and the land is rich in fruit and honey.

In both Norway and Sweden the winters are long and dark. But during the summer the sun can still be seen at midnight in the far North.

The meaning of the word 'Viking'

The Vikings were known by many different names. To the Franks they were simply known as the Northmen, while the English called them Danes. In Ireland they were *gaill*, or foreigners; in Germany they were *ashmen* because their ships were made from ashwood. In Eastern Europe they were called either **Varangians** or **Rus** — the modern Russians take their name from them.

The word *viking* itself comes from the **Old Norse** *vik*, meaning a narrow creek or inlet. A Viking was therefore a pirate who lay waiting in creeks and bays to attack passing ships.

A carved wooden animal's head found in the River Scheldt in the Low Countries. It was possibly either the figurehead of a Viking ship or part of a chieftain's high-seat.

The head of a Swedish chieftain, carved from elkhorn.

Viking Society

Viking society was divided into three different classes. At the top were the **jarls** or 'earls'. These were great and powerful chieftains who kept their own war-band of **housecarls** around them. Some jarls ruled over huge areas of land and were almost like kings; others owned nothing more than their longships but were widely admired and respected as leaders in battle.

Detail from the Bayeux Tapestry: two servants turning meat on a spit.

Most Vikings belonged to the 'freeman' class of **karls**. The typical karl was an independent farmer who owned his own land and was equal under the law to any other man. He might spend winter and spring at home tilling the soil, and summer away on a Viking expedition. Some karls were merchants or perhaps craftsmen such as blacksmiths, carpenters or shipwrights.

A wood carving of a rough peasant farmer, taken from the Oseberg cart in Norway.

The lowest class of all were **thralls** or 'slaves'. Slaves were either born into captivity or were captured during raids on foreign lands. They had few rights and could be bought or sold at their owners' whim. They were usually employed on farms or as servants in the home.

Things to do

Can You Remember?

1. What two things in particular do we remember the Vikings for?
2. In which years did the first two Viking raids on England take place? Where exactly were these raids?
3. Why should the Vikings attack monasteries like the one on Lindisfarne?
4. As a result of these attacks, what words did Christian priests cry out to God?
5. Which three countries did the Vikings come from?
6. Describe what each country was like. Why was it difficult to grow food in Scandinavia?
7. Why do you think that the Vikings took so readily to travelling by water?
8. Make a list of the various names by which the Vikings were known. Who called them by these names, and why?
9. Where does the word 'Viking' come from?
10. What were the three classes in Viking society?

Activities

1. Trace or copy the map of Scandinavia. Shade in the areas where it was easy to grow food.
2. Describe what is happening in the picture below.
3. Imagine that you were a monk living on Lindisfarne in A.D.793. Write a story about the Viking raid.

Group Project

Modern experts believe that, around A.D.800 the population of Scandinavia was growing quickly. Discuss in class why the Vikings suddenly started attacking foreign lands and settling there. Write down your ideas.

Vikings raiding a church and village.

2 Jarl the Chieftain

Let us go back to the years just after A.D.1000 when Sven Forkbeard was King of the Danes. At the head of a fjord in the island of Själland (pronounced *shaland*) stands a large Viking fortress.

It is circular in shape and surrounded by a high, earthen rampart. There are four, well-guarded gateways and a strong wooden palisade. Inside the fortress are four square barrack blocks. These are the living quarters of the men who guard the settlement.

On the shore of the fjord outside the rampart lie several longships. Groups of men are busily coating the ships' hulls with tar in readiness for a Viking raid abroad. Elsewhere warriors are shar-

pening spears, repairing shields and cleaning suits of chain mail. The clash of the blacksmith's hammer can be heard above the shouts of men at sword-practice.

The commander of the fortress is a man called Thorkel Haraldsson. He is known as Thorkel the Tall because of his great height. A Viking chief or nobleman is called a **jarl** (pronounced *yarl*). The word literally means 'warrior'.

Jarl Thorkel is the mightiest warrior in Denmark after King Sven himself. Every year he goes on Viking expeditions abroad and has become very rich with all the stolen treasure, or plunder, he has obtained. His luck in battle is so great that men are eager to follow his banner.

Thorkel's longhouse

During the winter months the seas are frozen over, so Thorkel stays at home with his men in his **longhouse**. They hunt during the day and feast at night in the Jarl's Great Hall.

But in the spring, once the ice has thawed, Thorkel has his ships made ready for sea. The Jarl and his warriors then sail abroad to plunder in foreign lands. A Viking cruise may last several months and it is not unknown for a ship's crew to be away from home for a year or more. During that time, they will have many adventures, battling against vast armies and besieging walled cities, to say nothing of the riches they might bring home with them.

Jarl Thorkel keeps a large number of warriors with him all the time. This is his 'war-band' and the members of it are his **housecarls**. The housecarls are proud to serve a man as famous as Thorkel. They have been specially chosen for their strength and courage.

When a man joins the Jarl's war band he swears an oath of loyalty to his master. He must never leave his side in battle but must protect his life to the very end. In return, the Jarl gives the housecarl food and shelter. Someone as wealthy as Thorkel the Tall also gives his men expensive gifts like rings and gold bracelets. And, of course, there is always the promise of plunder.

The Jarl

An Old Norse poem called the **Rigsthula** describes Jarl the Chieftain:

> Jarl had blond hair, bright cheeks and the piercing eyes of a young serpent. He spent his time constructing bows, hunting and riding to hounds, swimming and fencing. Jarl waged war, spurring his horse and reddening the land with the blood of his enemies.

We are also given a good idea of the life-style of a Viking jarl by the following passage from the **Orkneyinga Saga**:

> (The Jarl) would spend winter at home . . . where he kept eighty men at his own expense. His drinking-hall was so big that there was nothing (in the neighbourhood) to compare with it. In the spring, he was kept very busy, with much seed to sow. . . .
>
> . . . Then when that job was done, he would go off raiding on what he called his *spring-viking*, returning home just after midsummer, when he stayed until the cornfields had been harvested and the grain was safely stored. After that he would go off plundering again, not coming back until the first month of winter was over. This he called his *autumn-viking*.

The Nine Noble Skills

A Jarl was more than just a leader in battle. As a man of high birth he was expected to be skilled in all the noble pursuits of his class. The Nine Noble Skills were set out in a poem called the **Idrottir**.

Nine skills I have mastered —
I'm a champion at the chessboard:
Runes I seldom spoil,
I can read and write,
I'm skilled at skiing,
Shooting and rowing,
And what's more — I've learned
The harp and poetry.

Part of a Viking chess-set, made from walrus ivory.

The Runic Alphabet

Many Vikings were able to read and write. They used the **Futhark** or **Runic Alphabet**. Words written in the runic alphabet were called **runes**. Runes were often inscribed on warriors' swords or were carved on large stones in memory of the dead.

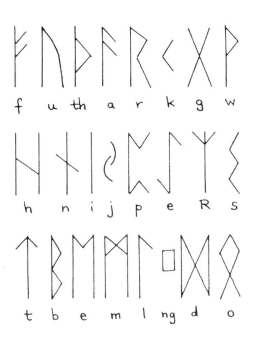

Viking names

A Viking took, as his surname, his or her father's first name. Thus, Bjorn, the son of Olaf, was called Bjorn Olafsson. His sister, Helga, would be Helga Olafsdotter.

The men of the North went in for colourful nicknames, also. Sven Forkbeard, King of the Danes, was named because of his habit of plaiting his long beard to prevent it from getting in his eyes. It didn't stop him from being defeated in battle by King Erik of the Swedes! Erik became known as Erik the Victorious. But Sven had the last laugh: he stole Erik's wife, Sigrid. She was known as Sigrid the Haughty because of her overbearing manner.

Eyvind the Braggart boasted a lot; Rolf Ganger (the Walker) went everywhere on foot since he was too heavy to ride a horse; Valgard the Grey had grey hair; Olaf the Peacock loved fine clothes. Harald Hardrada was the 'hard ruler' defeated at the Battle of Stamford Bridge.

Erik Bloodaxe, one-time King of York, was named thus from the ferocity with which he removed his rivals for power. But one of the strangest of nicknames was possessed by Ivar the Boneless. It was said that, as the result of a curse placed on his parents' wedding-night, his body was made of gristle instead of bone.

11

Aerial view of the Viking fortress at Trelleborg, Själland, built sometime between A.D.960 and 1000.

Things to do

Can You Remember?

1. What did the word 'Jarl' literally mean?
2. Why were so many men willing to serve under Thorkel the Tall?
3. Why did Vikings often not go raiding in winter or midsummer?
4. What was a war-band? What were the men who formed it known as?
5. According to the Rigsthula, what sort of occupations did the Jarl have?
6. What were the Nine Noble Skills?
7. What were runes?
8. How do you think the Futhark got its name?
9. If people had the same sort of surnames today as they had in Viking times, what would you be called?
10. Think of some famous people today. What sort of nicknames might the Vikings give them?

Activities

1. Write a paragraph describing the various activities followed by the Jarl and his war-band during the year.
2. Copy out the Runic Alphabet. Then write your own name in runes.
3. Describe the Viking fortress in the picture above. Why would it be difficult for an enemy to get inside?

Group Project

Construct your own model Viking fortress. The earthen ramparts could be made from clay or plaster; the wooden palisade from used matchsticks, and the longhouses from card or paper.

3 Vikings at War

The Jarl's ships have now been repainted and fitted with new sails. His warriors check their equipment and load it on board. At last the expedition is ready to set sail.

But, first, they must make a sacrifice to **Aegir**, the sea-god. Thorkel orders that a sheep be slaughtered on the deck of his own ship and then thrown overboard. When this is done, a large flock of seagulls suddenly appears. The Vikings think this to be a good omen, for they are very superstitious, and they set off in high spirits.

It is Thorkel the Tall's custom to travel eastwards to the lands of the Obotrites and Wends. The tribes here are wild and uncivilised. Their villages are usually laden with treasure taken in attacks further south on Saxon towns. A successful raid will also yield plenty of prisoners who can then be sold as slaves.

But, recently, these people have learned to defend themselves against the Vikings. Their villages lie behind strong fortifications so it is very difficult to get inside. Therefore, plenty of hard fighting lies ahead for Jarl Thorkel and his men.

Weapons and Armour

Viking warriors fought with a wide variety of weapons — swords, spears, axes, bows and arrows.

The **sword** was the aristocrat among weapons, much favoured by chieftains. Much expense was involved in obtaining one and many were imported into Scandinavia from Saxony and Gaul. One famous swordsmith called Ulfberht, who lived in the Rhineland, signed his name on the tops of his blades, many of which have been found in Viking graves.

The Vikings considered swords to possess magical qualities. Legends were told of them having been forged by dwarves. Many had names, engraved in runes on the blade, like *Quernbiter*, *Whitefire* and *Fish-spine*.

Viking swords were often double-edged and had a **blood-channel** which was a groove running down the middle on both sides of the blade. This was to help balance it and the **pommel** on the end of the hilt was weighted for the same purpose.

Even more fearsome than the sword was the **axe**. There were two basic types: the **bearded axe**, named from the drooping point, or beard, which hung from its lower edge; and the **broad axe** which had a long curved blade. Both were deadly weapons, capable of inflicting terrible wounds.

The **Laxdale Saga** gives a bloodthirsty account of a battle involving the use of several types of weapon:

An Brushwood-Stomach burst into the **shieling** with his shield over his head . . . Bolle lunged at him with *Legbiter*, slicing through the side of his shield and cleaving his skull to the shoulders. An died immediately.

Then Lambe Thorbjornsson went in. He held a shield in front of him and carried a drawn sword. At that moment, Bolle was pulling *Legbiter* out of An's body and his shield had slipped to one side. Lambe struck at Bolle's thigh and wounded him badly. Bolle slashed back at Lambe's shoulder and the sword ripped down his side. . . .

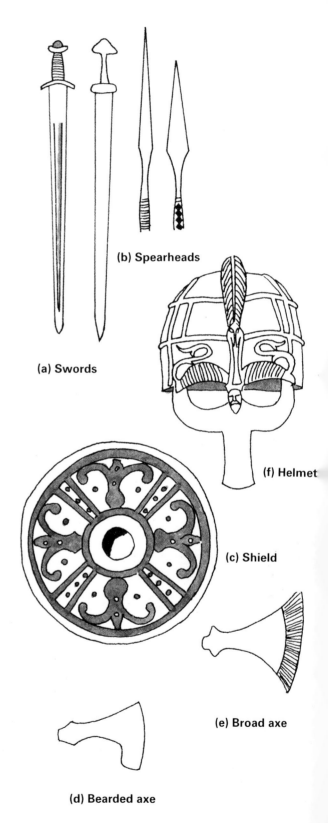

(a) Swords

(b) Spearheads

(f) Helmet

(c) Shield

(e) Broad axe

(d) Bearded axe

A Danish axe-head. The design on the blade was gouged out with a hammer and chisel, then filled in with strips of silver

Then Helge Hardbeinsson went into the shieling, carrying a spear with a blade 18 inches (45 centimetres) long and an iron-bound shaft.

Helge thrust at Bolle with the spear; it went right through his shield and through Bolle himself. . . .

Bolle was still leaning against the wall of the shieling, clutching his tunic tightly to stop his guts falling out. Steinthor Olafsson then sprang at him and, swinging a great axe at his neck just above the shoulders, caused his head to fly off at once.

Wealthy Vikings, and the housecarls of great chieftains, often wore coats of chain mail called **byrnies**. Others made do with a heavy leather jerkin.

Helmets could be made from iron or leather and were either round or conical in shape.

The following extract from the sagas gives some idea of the awesome sight of a Viking warrior in full battle-gear:

He was so tall that no one came higher than up to his shoulders. He was very handsome in appearance, with a fine head of blond hair. He was well armed with a beautiful helmet, chain mail armour and a red shield. In his belt was a superb sword and, in his hand, a gilded spear, the shaft of which was so thick that it was a handful to grasp.

Berserkers and Ulfhednars

Berserkers were described as men who charged without ring armour (chain mail) and were like mad dogs and wolves. They bit the rims of their shields and possessed the strength of bears and wildboars. They were impervious to fire and steel.

Other warriors, called **Ulfhednars** dressed for battle in wolfskins.

Both berserkers and ulfhednars were greatly prized as housecarls by kings and jarls. Their almost insane courage and recklessness terrified the enemy, at the same time giving confidence to their own comrades. But in times of peace, they were not so popular and the sagas tell many stories of berserkers who were outlawed for violence towards their neighbours.

Towns and Sieges

The sagas give many accounts of Vikings besieging castles and fortified towns. Occasionally, the attackers would hit upon clever tricks in order to get inside the defences: such as capturing birds which had their nests within the fortress, and tying splinters of tarred wood onto their backs. The splinters were then set alight and the birds would fly back inside the walls and onto the thatched roofs of the buildings and set fire to them. Another idea was to dig underground passages beneath the walls of a town and up into the living quarters of the unsuspecting defenders.

One of the most original plans involved an army of Vikings who put up the flag of truce and asked whether their leader, who had just died, could be given a Christian burial within the city walls. The funeral procession was duly allowed through the gates and into the cathedral. Once inside, the lid of the coffin was suddenly thrown aside as the 'dead' chieftain, now miraculously brought back to life, emerged sword in hand to cut down the bishop at his altar.

More often, the Vikings had to resort to more conventional means in order to capture walled towns. Here is a contemporary account of the Siege of Paris in A.D.885:

The Northmen built three enormous siege machines out of huge oak trees, lashed together and mounted on sixteen wheels. A battering ram was fixed up inside each machine, covered by a wooden roof. Sixty men hid inside each one.

They shot thousands of lead balls from slings into the town, and powerful catapults fired at the walls.

Thorkel's Expedition

Thorkel the Tall's expedition has not gone well. His warriors have attacked three villages, but with poor results. The first two were poorly defended but the Vikings' plunder consisted only of a few sides of smoked pork and some roughly made farming implements.

Thorkel's men then attacked the stronghold of a powerful Wendish chief. After fierce fighting, during which many of the Jarl's best housecarls were killed, the village was eventually taken. But the fleeing inhabitants first set fire to wooden buildings so that any possible plunder was destroyed.

To make things worse, two of Thorkel's ships have been wrecked by a

A Viking ship full of armed warriors engraved on a Gotland picture-stone.

heavy storm on the way home. It is, therefore, with an ill humour that the Jarl moors his vessel to the jetty outside the fortress and steps ashore.

Things to Do

Can You Remember?
1. Before setting off on a Viking expedition, Thorkel the Tall's men made a sacrificial offering to one of the gods. Which god did they sacrifice to, and why?
2. Make a list of weapons used by the Vikings in battle.
3. Who was Ulfberht, and how do we know about him?
4. The groove running down the middle of the sword's blade was sometimes called the 'blood-channel'. How do you think it got this name? What was the groove's real purpose?
5. What was the difference between the 'bearded axe' and the 'broad axe'?
6. The knob in the centre of a shield was called the **boss**. Can you think of two purposes it had?
7. What was a 'byrnie'? Why would owning one be very expensive?
8. In battle, the Vikings often used a formation known as the **shield-ring**. What do you imagine this was?
9. The word 'berserker' is derived from the Old Norse: *ber* meaning bare (or possibly bear) and *sark* meaning shirt or tunic. What, therefore, does 'berserker' literally mean?
10. What was an 'ulfhednar'?

Activities
1. Make a chart entitled *'Viking Weapons and Armour'*.
2. Describe three tricks which the Vikings occasionally used in order to get inside an enemy town or fortress.
3. Write a story about Thorkel the Tall's attack on the village in Wendland.

Group Project
The Vikings used a special siege machine during the Siege of Paris. Construct a model of the machine described on page 16 from pieces of wood, cork and cardboard.

4 The Feast and the Chase

Thorkel the Tall is a man who lives for war. No sooner has he arrived home than he is planning his next voyage. But much of his time is spent enjoying his favourite pastime, that of hunting. Mounted on horseback and armed only with stout spears, the Jarl and his housecarls follow and chase the deer and wild boar which live in the heaths and woods surrounding the fortress.

Occasionally, Thorkel goes hawking instead. This is a very popular sport among the men of the North and to own a good bird is the ambition of many a Viking. Thorkel, himself, has a beautiful white Greenland Falcon which he bought from a merchant in Hedeby.

While Thorkel is out hunting or visiting his farms, his wife, Gudrun, is busy supervising the work in the kitchen of his **Great Hall**. Since the fortress is a military settlement, the only women allowed inside the rampart are members of the Jarl's own family and household servants.

As lady of the Jarl's household, it is Gudrun's duty to see that meals are prepared on time for her husband and his housecarls. This is no easy job since over sixty people eat and sleep in the Hall itself.

The kitchen stands at one end of the Hall. The air is thick with smoke from the large open hearth. Kitchen-maids

The very rare Greenland Falcon, much prized among the northern peoples.

hurry to and fro carrying buckets of water while others cut up meat on huge oak tables, or stir stew in large iron cauldrons.

Gudrun's form of relaxation is to retire to the **bower** at the other end of the hall with the other women of the household. Here, they sit and chat together while spinning, weaving and embroidering cloth. Sometimes they work at weaving a tapestry to hang in the Hall and keep out cold draughts. Some of these tapestries tell stories about the Vikings' gods. Others show hunting and battle scenes.

Viking longhouse of the Trelleborg type.

Horse-fighting

Horse-fighting was very popular among wealthy Vikings. Two stallions would be provoked into combat by their owners, by *goading* them with a sharp stick, or *goad*, usually in the presence of a mare. The winner was eventually declared when one of the stallions was severely injured or just lost interest in the fight. Occasionally, as the following extract from **Njal's Saga** shows, horse-fighting could result in violent quarrels breaking out between the owners themselves:

The horses started fighting and bit each other for a long time without needing to be goaded. It was excellent sport. Then Thorgeir and Koll planned to give their own horse a shove when they next charged at each other, to see if they could knock Gunnar over.

The horses clashed again, and Thorgeir and Koll gave a mighty heave against their horse's rump. But Gunnar gave his own horse a push, forcing Thorgeir and Koll onto their backs with their horse on top of them. . . .

Thorgeir struck Gunnar's horse, blinding it in one eye. Gunnar hit Thorgeir with the goad and Thorgeir fell unconscious.

In the Great Hall

The noisiest time of day is undoubtedly the evening. Now, the Jarl, together with his family and housecarls, assemble in the Great Hall for the main meal of the day.

Many travellers pass nearby the fortress. If they require food and shelter for the night, a place will be found for them inside one of the longhouses. Really important guests are fed and entertained in the Great Hall itself. A great nobleman like Thorkel the Tall prides himself on being more hospitable than other men.

When the Jarl's household have all assembled, the food is served. Servants bring in strong-smelling shoulder pork on long-forked spits, bubbling troughs of blood-sausage and clay platters filled with bread-cakes and sweetmeats. A butt of ale is also provided at each table for the men to fill their tankards and drinking-horns.

The Vikings have to make their own entertainment in the evenings. Jugglers and acrobats perform feats of skill up and down the long aisles between tables. By the High Seat, where the Jarl sits with the most important members of his household, a **skald**, or poet, tells stories to the music of a harp.

These stories, called **sagas**, of gods and heroes are very popular. The whole company listens quietly as the skald finishes his tale. If it is a good story, the Jarl will give its teller a present, perhaps a silver armlet. Good poets are highly valued here in the North.

The feast ends with a great drinking bout. A Viking considers himself a fine fellow if he is still above the table at the end of the evening. The men of the North are a boastful people, but never more so than when drinking. They argue about who is the bravest warrior among them, or else they swear oaths to perform great feats of courage once they are sober again.

Finally, when only a soft glow is seen from the fires in the Great Hall, the company staggers from the drinking benches onto the straw-lined floor. There, they lie down to sleep with the hounds until morning.

In the Bower

The picture above shows Gudrun with the other women of the household in the bower of the Great Hall. Gudrun herself, seated on the left, is spinning woollen thread. In her left hand is a wooden stick called a **distaff**, at one end of which is the unspun wool. From this, she gently teases the fibres onto a weighted **spindle-whorl**.

The woman on the far right is weaving the spun wool into cloth on a **warp-weighted loom**. The vertical threads (warp) are held taut by soapstone weights. Working from the top down, the horizontal threads (weft) are passed through the gap in the warp and then beaten upwards again.

Spinning and weaving were among the most important tasks performed by Viking women. As well as clothes, they had to make tents, awnings, ships' sails and tapestries to hang on walls.

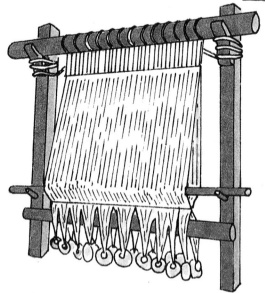

A warp-weighted loom. These were still in use as recently as the nineteenth century in the Faroe Islands.

The oaths are sworn, the warriors rest.

Things to Do

Can You Remember?

1. Mention three pastimes popular among Viking chiefs.
2. What exactly is hawking?
3. What tasks were performed by the women of the household?
4. Where did the women make cloth?
5. Describe in detail how wool was spun and woven.
6. What is a tapestry? Can you name a famous example?
7. Make a list of the kinds of food served to the Jarl and his housecarls.
8. How did the Vikings entertain themselves in the evenings?
9. What was a 'skald'? How was he rewarded for his skill?
10. How was the floor of the Great Hall covered? Can you think of a reason for this?

Activities

1. Make a picture chart, illustrating and describing the various tasks and pastimes performed by the members of the Jarl's household.

2. Describe the scene shown in the picture on page 20.
3. Make two lists of the forms of recreation and entertainment indulged in by the Vikings and those enjoyed by yourself. What are the main differences.?

Group Project

Most libraries have books relating the old Icelandic sagas, many of which were popular in Viking times. Read one together in class.

Detail from a tapestry.

5 Karl the Freeman

There are only a few great chieftains like Thorkel the Tall in the North. Most Vikings are simple farmers, called **karls**. A karl is a 'freeman'. He owes services to no other man, owns his land and is equal in the eyes of the law to all other men, high or low.

Toke Gudbrandsson is a prosperous farmer from Skania in southern Sweden. As a young man, Toke (pronounced *tok-er*) went on Viking raids abroad. He returned with plunder taken in the lands of the Saxons and the Franks. As the eldest son, he inherited the family farm when his father died. He was then rich enough to build a larger longhouse with new barns and sheds for his crops and livestock. Toke is known as Toke of Geirstad from the name of his farm.

The inhabitants of those areas near the coast live together in large villages for protection against pirates — Vikings attack one another as well as people in foreign lands. But it is safer farther inland and here, at Geirstad, Toke lives some distance from his neighbours.

He is a well-respected man locally, renowned for the open house he keeps for friend and stranger alike. No hungry traveller need fear being turned away without a full meal and shelter for the night. But Toke is not popular with the men who work for him. He is a mean and hard task-master. His **thralls** (slaves) have learned to fear his temper and the rod he carries with him in the fields.

Toke's wife is called Freydis. She is a proud, harsh-voiced woman but a good housekeeper. They have five sons and three daughters.

The eldest son is called Orm. His name means *Serpent*. Orm is an able young man and will take over the farm one day. But his brothers will have to look elsewhere for land. Grim, the second son, knows men who have 'gone a-Viking' in England and found land to settle on there. He intends to do the same as soon as a suitable opportunity presents itself.

Toke's daughters have two roles in life. One is to help their mother look after the longhouse, and to cook and make cloth. The second is to make good marriages with the sons of other rich farmers. This will give Toke of Geirstad a reputation as a man of importance.

The Karl

The vast majority of Vikings belonged to the 'freeman' class of peasant-farmers. Most of these were small-holders, occupying a single farmhouse together with their families and livestock, and just a single field. A few were more prosperous, with extensive farmsteads and broad estates. A description of Karl the Freeman is found in the **Rigsthula**:

> Karl was red-haired, ruddy and bright-eyed. Eagerly he set to work, breaking oxen, making ploughs and building timber houses. Karl raised barns, constructed carts and followed the plough.

Although such men were free and equal under the law, in practice, they were dominated by neighbouring noblemen and chieftains. In times of trouble and at **things** (local assemblies), they were expected to unite behind their chieftain and, in return, he would protect them against their enemies.

But a Viking's fiercest loyalty was to his own family and kinsfolk. In a harsh and violent world, it was vital that the members of a family stick together at all times. A small quarrel between two men or, worse, a murder, would frequently result in an endless **blood-feud** between families as they attempted to avenge their kinsmen.

The Viking Code

The Vikings' world was often unfriendly and dangerous. A man learned to take life as it came, to value his friends and guard against his enemies. An Icelandic poem called the **Havamal** served as advice for young men during this daily struggle:

When a guest arrives chilled to the bone from crossing the mountains, he needs fire, food and clothing.

Be careful, but not too careful; be most careful with ale and other men's wives. Beware also of thieves.

Praise no day until evening, no wife until she is dead, no sword until tested, no maid until married, no ice until crossed, no ale until it is drunk.

A coward thinks he will live forever if he avoids battle; but old age catches up with all men.

Cattle die, kinsfolk die, we shall all die one day. But one thing will never die — the reputation a man leaves behind him.

A guest should not outstay his welcome; even a friend becomes disliked if he lingers too long in the hall of his host.

A man ought never to leave his weapons when out in the fields, since he never knows when he will require his spear.

A man who plans on taking his neighbour's life and property should get up early. A wolf in its lair never catches food, nor a sleeping man victory.

Do not deceive a friend. A lost friend brings a man sadness.

The wealthiest man is he who has a good store of common sense.

A man should be wise but not too wise. He who cannot forsee his fate is happiest.

It is a fool who lies awake at night worrying; for when morning comes he is tired and his troubles are the same as they were before.

Ale is not good for a man: the more he drinks the less control he has of his wits.

The Vikings felt that, however wisely or carefully a man behaved, eventually his fate would be decided by how lucky he was. A chieftain who was skilled in the arts of war might, nevertheless, gain a reputation for being unlucky. Others would be reluctant to follow him into battle. A sea-captain renowned for his bad weather-luck would find no crews to man his ships. Good luck was considered the greatest gift that the gods could bestow.

25

Women were rarely allowed to give evidence in front of a jury and their husbands were held responsible for their actions. For most of them, life was a constant round of household chores, child-rearing and the milking of cattle.

The picture on the left shows what might be a typical woman of the period: the wife of a freeman such as Toke of Geirstad. She is holding a **distaff** with which to spin woollen thread (an almost endless task) and sewing implements are pinned onto her apron. The keys fastened to her waist are a badge of her position as mistress of the household. Her hair, like that of most housewives, is gathered under a knotted headscarf. Girls and unmarried women wore their hair loose and flowing. Marriages

A ninth-century Norwegian oak bed. When in use, it would have been covered with a mattress and eiderdown quilt.

Viking Women

Compared to those living elsewhere in Europe, Viking women enjoyed a great amount of freedom and independence. They were able to own land, inherit property and even divorce their husbands if they wished. The sagas tell of many women who had such great power and influence that their actions resulted in blood-feuds between families.

However, in most ways, women were treated very much as inferiors by their menfolk. The following verse from the **Havamal** illustrates how they were viewed by the opposite sex:

No man should trust the words of a girl or a housewife; since their hearts have been shaped on a turning wheel and they are changeable by nature.

were usually made in order to unite different families. Girls were expected to fall in with their parents' wishes. The groom paid a sum of money called the **bride-price** which his new wife kept for herself. She was also given a **dowry** by her father of useful goods or money to bring to her new home. The marriage ceremony took place during the festivities which followed and involved drinking the *bridal ale*.

Wealthy Vikings frequently kept a number of mistresses at home as well as their wives, and often had children by them. But if a woman committed adultery, she and her lover could be punished by death.

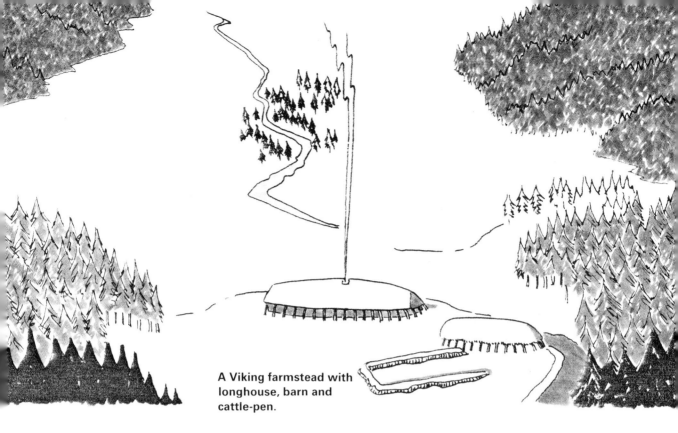

A Viking farmstead with longhouse, barn and cattle-pen.

Things to Do

Can you Remember?

1. What did it mean to be a karl, or freeman?
2. According to the Rigsthula, what kind of life did a karl lead?
3. What caused a blood-feud?
4. Why do you imagine that the Vikings thought hospitality towards travellers so important?
5. Mention two things which were considered essential to get a man through life.
6. What was a young man advised to be careful of?
7. How were Viking women regarded by their menfolk?
8. How did housewives differ in their dress and appearance from unmarried women?
9. What were the bride-price and dowry?
10. Compare the way in which Viking law treated men on the one hand and women on the other.

Activities

1. Write a short story which illustrates the advice given in the Havamal.
2. Trace or copy the picture of the Viking housewife. Label the various items of her clothes and equipment.
3. How did the marriage customs of the Vikings differ from your own family's?

Group Project

Discuss in class the Viking code. How well would it fit our own society?

Detail from the Bayeux Tapestry. The native horse of Scandinavia was little more than a pony but was very tough and able to survive the cold in the North.

6 Life on the Land

Good farming land in Scandinavia is scarce. To the west, in Norway, it is too mountainous. In Denmark, the soil is thin and sandy. Much of the rest of Scandinavia is covered with thick forest. Here in Skania, however, at Geirstad, conditions are better. The soil is good, the hills not too steep and, though the winters are long and cold, the summers are hot and sunny — just right for ripening fields of wheat and rye.

Toke Gudbrandsson's farmstead is situated at the head of a fertile valley, not far from the River Helge (Holy River). As well as growing cereals, he keeps many cattle and sheep. The surrounding forest is rich in game while the river is full of fish and waterfowl of all varieties.

The Vikings build their homes from whatever materials are available locally. Timber houses can be seen almost everywhere in Scandinavia due to the plentiful supply of trees. Those who have settled in the barren, windswept islands of the North Atlantic, such as the Orkneys or Iceland, must make do with turf and stone.

Toke's farmstead consists of two timbered buildings: a longhouse where he and his family eat and sleep, and a barn for his crops. Some distance away stands a cattle-shed. Other less prosperous farmers just have a single building in which they live side-by-side with their livestock.

Toke employs several other men on his land. Some of them are freemen like himself. They are paid wages for their work but also live under the same roof as their master and his family. Toke has a number of **thralls** as well. These are slaves who are their master's personal property and have few rights of their own.

The gods play a great part in the lives of the local community. No task is undertaken without saying prayers or sacrificing to **Frey** the god of fertility, and **Thor** the god of good weather.

If the gods are pleased with them, the harvest will be a plentiful one.

The Farming Year

Winter was a quiet season on the land. Hours of daylight were short and the Vikings preferred to huddle round their log fires. But they did venture out to fell trees for timber. Since there was no sap in the trees in winter, the wood was drier and easier to cut.

With autumn and the shorter evenings, sheep and cattle were brought down from their summer pastures. A few were chosen to be kept alive for the following year. The rest were slaughtered and salted to feed the farming community during the long, cold months ahead.

With the coming of spring and the melting of the winter snows, the land could be ploughed and seeds sown.

During the summer, grass was cut and dried for hay. Later, iron sickles and scythes were used to reap the harvest of wheat, barley or rye.

We are given many descriptions of life on the land in the sagas. For instance, the **Laxdale Saga** tells of a farmer called Olaf:

Some distance from Hoskuldstead . . . a clearing had been cut in the forest, and you could be certain to find Olaf's livestock gathered there, in good weather or bad. One autumn Olaf had a farmhouse built in that same clearing, using timber hewn from the forest, as well as driftwood.

The first winter that Olaf lived (there) he had many thralls and farmhands, each of whom had a particular job to do. One of them looked after the barren cattle, and another the *milch* (milking) cows. The cow byre was out in the forest some distance from the farmhouse.

The Craftsman

Travel overland was difficult in Viking times. Goods could not easily be transported from far away and, therefore, villages and farmsteads had to be self-sufficient in food and the other necessities of life. Farmers often doubled as craftsmen, supplying themselves and their neighbours with wooden and metal hardware. The following verse tells something of the blacksmith's skill and energy:

Look, a smith who wants wealth
Will leave his bed at dawn
And force awake the bright flames
Of his slumbering fire.
Then hammers will sing,
Crash on red-hot iron,
And wind-starved bellows will
Whine, draw air, wheeze and scream.

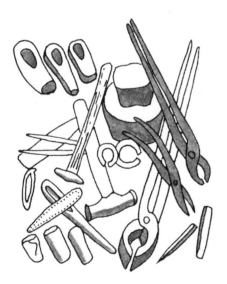

Food and Cooking

Vikings ate two meals a day: morning and evening. Their food was usually plain, consisting of wheaten or rye breadcakes, oatmeal porridge, fish, beef, mutton, pork and goats' meat. They drank milk, beer, mead (a brew made from honey) and occasionally wine which the wealthy imported from abroad.

Food was cooked over a large, open fire in the middle of the longhouse, either by being roasted on a spit or boiled in large, iron cauldrons.

Hunting and Fishing

Among the wealthy, hunting was more a sport than a necessity. Others, however, were forced to supplement their produce obtained from farming by chasing and snaring game. The forests teemed with wildlife, including elk, deer, wildboar and bear.

Nearer the coast, fishing was a major occupation. Men rowed out to sea to catch, not only herring and cod, but even large mammals such as whales and seals.

A collection of buckets, ladles and cooking utensils taken from the Oseberg ship-burial, Norway.

Clothes and Appearance

The Vikings were fond of brightly-coloured clothes. For men, the normal form of dress was a woollen tunic reaching to the knee. They also wore breeches with leather cross-garters, and boots. Cloaks, and sometimes hats, were worn in cold weather and were made from either wool or thick fur.

Even in peacetime, a freeman would rarely be without his sword. But it was considered a provocative act to draw it from its scabbard.

During the Viking period, it was the custom for men to let their beard grow but, like their hair, it was kept neatly trimmed.

Women wore two rectangular pieces of cloth, front and back, over a long, linen undergarment. Occasionally, drawers or stockings were worn underneath. Housewives kept their hair gathered up beneath a knotted headscarf.

Both men and women were very fond of expensive jewellery. This was usually obtained in raids abroad but Viking goldsmiths were also able to produce magnificently worked bracelets, brooches and rings.

Children and Growing Up

Children were brought up far more strictly than nowadays. Disobedience was frequently dealt with by severe beatings for boys and girls alike. Even so, a headstrong, manly spirit was admired and encouraged in a young Viking boy.

When a baby was born, it was examined by its father. Weaklings were immediately put out to die. A healthy infant, however, was sprinkled with water, named and given a present.

Children did not go to school. Boys were taught farming and craftsmanship: they also learned to write **runes** and handle weapons. Girls helped their mothers in the longhouse and milking-parlour.

A boy came of age at sixteen. From then on, he was considered a man and was expected to fight if the community came under attack. But he would not normally marry until he reached his early twenties.

Things to Do

Can You Remember?

1. Explain why Geirstad was such a suitable place for Toke Gudbrandsson to have his farm.
2. Why were the gods so important in the lives of Viking farmers?
3. Why did tree-felling take place in winter-time?
4. What were sickles and scythes used for? Draw pictures of them.
5. How were slaughtered livestock preserved through the winter?
6. What does 'self-sufficient' mean?
7. How did the Vikings obtain food apart from by farming?
8. Draw pictures showing food being roasted and boiled.
9. Explain what happened when a baby was born.
10. When did a Viking boy come of age? What was then expected of him?

Activities

1. Write a paragraph describing the various activities which occupied the farming community throughout the year.
2. Make a chart entitled *Carpenters and Smiths*. Draw separately each of the tools illustrated on page 30, label them and explain their use.
3. Trace or copy the pictures on page 31 showing Viking costume. Label each item of clothing.

Group Project

Make a frieze for your classroom wall with the theme *Life on the Land*. Groups of pupils can illustrate and write about the following activities: tree-felling, hunting, fishing, carpentry, metal-working, ploughing, sowing, harvesting and slaughtering.

The evening meal.

7 Thrall the Slave

Rapp Crookback is a slave. He has always been a slave. His parents were also slaves and so were their parents before them.

Rapp is the property of Toke Gudbrandsson. He used to belong to another farmer but was sold because he was so clumsy and kept causing accidents. His previous owner had a bad temper and often beat him. The end came when Rapp let some sheep out of their pen by mistake. They knocked over some buckets of milk and began to eat a crop of barley.

Rapp was sorely whipped when his master found out. Then he was locked in a shed for three days without food or water. Finally, he was put in a cart along with the livestock and taken to the market-town of Hedeby.

There were many other slaves sold that day. Rapp noticed that some of them spoke with a strange, foreign language. Someone said that they had been taken prisoner in a Viking raid on the coast of Ireland. There were also a couple of very beautiful, dark-skinned girls with black hair and flashing white teeth. They had been captured from a land far to the south where, it was said, very few northerners had ventured.

The two girls were the first to be sold. They fetched a good price — fifty pieces of silver — from a very old, but very wealthy, chieftain. Rapp nearly wasn't sold at all. No one seemed willing to buy him because of his skinny appearance. In the end, the slave-dealer was forced to settle for a very low price — two iron bars and a leather belt.

That was twenty years ago when Rapp was fifteen. Since then, he has worked on Toke's farm at Geirstad. He sleeps at night on a rough bed of straw at one end of the cattle-shed with the other thralls. His meals consist of two bowls of gruel a day or, on rare occasions, tripe.

Rapp has thought of escaping but the question is *where?* The world outside is as harsh and hostile as the farm is unpleasant. Runaway slaves are easily recognisable and, if not returned to their own master, will be resold to someone else. In any case, the forest is full of wolves and bears. It is unlikely that a man would get far before he either starved to death or became a meal for some other hungry creature.

But Rapp's life is not entirely without hope. He is allowed to grow some crops of his own and sell them at a profit. One day, he hopes to save enough money to buy his freedom.

The Thrall

Slaves or thralls, formed the lowest class in Viking society. It is possible that many of them were descended from the original inhabitants of Scandinavia who were conquered by tall, blond invaders from the East. For countless generations, they and their families lived as slaves. The **Rigsthula** describes a thrall as being:

> black and ugly with rough hands, knotted knuckles and thick fingers. His back was hunched and his feet flat. Thrall was set to work building fences, manuring fields, tending pigs, guarding goats and digging peat. The whole day long he carried great loads of firewood.

It was also possible for people to be condemned to slavery as a punishment for criminal offences. Others might sell themselves in order to pay off a debt.

Many slaves were obtained in Viking raids abroad. When the Island of Walcheren, off the Frisian coast, was attacked in A.D.837 many women were led away in chains. An Irishman living at about the same time wrote of his countrymen being carried off 'over the broad green sea'. The Vikings themselves suffered the same fate at the hands of their enemies. When the Irish captured the Viking town of Dublin in A.D.1000, it was said that 'no man would wield a flail, nor would a woman grind flour, knead a cake or wash clothes, but had a foreign (Viking) man or woman to work for them.'

The lot of the slave

As one might expect, slaves were treated with scorn and contempt by other sections of society. This is clear from the **Rigsthula** which gives the sons of Thrall names like *Brawler*, *Cattle-man*, *Clumsy*, *Ugly* and *Clot*. Their sisters are called *Clump*, *Fat-legs*, *Hook-nose*, *Fish-wife* and *Torn-skirt*.

They were given all the most unpleasant jobs to do. The men worked in the fields and tended livestock while the women were engaged in corn-grinding, dairying, washing and cooking.

Slaves were not allowed to carry weapons. Their hair was cut very short and they normally wore a plain tunic of white, un-dyed wool. They had no legal rights and if one were injured, compensation was paid, not to him, but to his master. Their treatment varied from owner to owner. Some were no doubt badly treated. On the other hand, many slaves, especially household servants, must have been looked on almost as members of the family.

One wealthy landowner called Erling Skjalgsson had thirty slaves on his farm:

(Erling) would allot the day's work to his slaves, but would then give them their time free, allowing every man who so wished to work for himself in the evening and at night.

He gave them some land to sow corn for themselves, and let them sell it for their own profit. He would give a particular amount of work to each man, to win himself freedom by doing it . . . and all who wished to work could make themselves free within three years.

Unfortunately, it is probable that men like Erling were the exception rather than the rule.

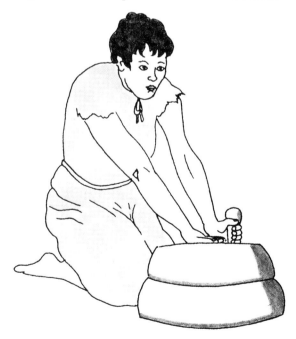

A shipment of slaves being sold on the quayside.

Things to Do

Can You Remember?

1. What exactly is a slave?
2. Mention four ways in which the Vikings obtained their slaves.
3. Read the description of Thrall from the Rigsthula. Why do you think he looked like that?
4. What sorts of jobs were done by slaves?
5. Look through the names of Thrall's sons and daughters. What does this tell us about the Vikings' attitude towards slaves?
6. How could slaves be recognised?
7. In what way did the law distinguish between slaves and free men?
8. Why was it so difficult to escape from slavery?
9. How else could a man obtain his freedom?
10. What is the woman on page 35 doing?

Activities

1. Nowadays we accept that slavery is evil and inhumane. Why might it also be an unsatisfactory system from the owner's point of view?
2. Describe in detail the scene shown above.
3. Imagine that you were a slave on Toke Gudbrandsson's farm. Describe your escape and the adventures which follow.

Group Project

Read more about the history of slavery up to the twentieth century.

8 Towns and Traders

Most freemen are farmers like Toke of Geirstad. A few, however, make their living as merchants and traders, sailing to far off lands in order to do honest business with the native inhabitants. Amund Amundsson, a Norwegian from Halogaland in the far North, is such a man.

Each spring, Amund sets out in his **knorr**, or trading-ship, for the South. On board, he takes a cargo of hides, walrus ivory and salted fish. His crew, though not on a Viking expedition, are well-armed and picked for their fighting ability. The fjords along the coast are infested with pirates who attack passing merchant vessels which might have valuable cargoes.

Amund plots his course for the Danish market-town of Hedeby, a great trading-centre for all the peoples of the North.

From throughout the known world, merchants come to Hedeby to sell their wares: fair-haired Frisian men with boatloads of wheat, wool and sword-blades; dark-skinned Arabs from the South, carrying spices, wine and furs, honey and slaves. Viking fleets also sail to Hedeby to unload their plunder.

There is a great demand for the goods Amund Amundsson has to sell. Ivory, in particular, fetches a high price on account of its rareness and is used to make such items as sword-handles and bishops' croziers or staffs! In return, Amund buys luxury articles to take home with him; expensive oriental silks, glass beakers from the Rhineland and Moorish silverware.

Merchants in Danger

Not all voyages are profitable. On three occasions, Amund has been shipwrecked in stormy seas. The last time out he was chased by Vikings and only escaped their clutches by throwing his merchandise overboard, thereby lightening his ship. Other men he knows have fared even worse. One crew, carrying a shipment of slaves, were attacked by their cargo, overpowered and sold at the very market-place they were bound for!

Despite the dangers of his calling, however, Amund Amundsson is not yet ready to retire. He finds the unpredictable nature of his life far preferable to the boring labours of the ploughman. Besides, the merchant's profession is greatly honoured in the North. And honour, together with good luck, is the most valuable of possessions.

Hedeby — a Viking Market Town

Here is the market town of Hedeby as it might have appeared in the early eleventh century. A semi-circular rampart and wooden palisade offer protection against attack by land. A *mole*, or causeway, extends into the harbour for ships to tie up to.

Around A.D.950, an Arab visitor to Hedeby described the town like this:

> There are freshwater wells in the town. The local inhabitants are heathens, except for a few Christians who have a church there. . . . The town is poor in goods and treasure. The main diet of the inhabitants is fish, which is very plentiful there. When a child is born, they often cast it into the sea to save expense. . . . I have never heard such awful singing as that of the townsmen of Hedeby: it is like a growl coming out of their throats, like the howling of dogs, only worse.

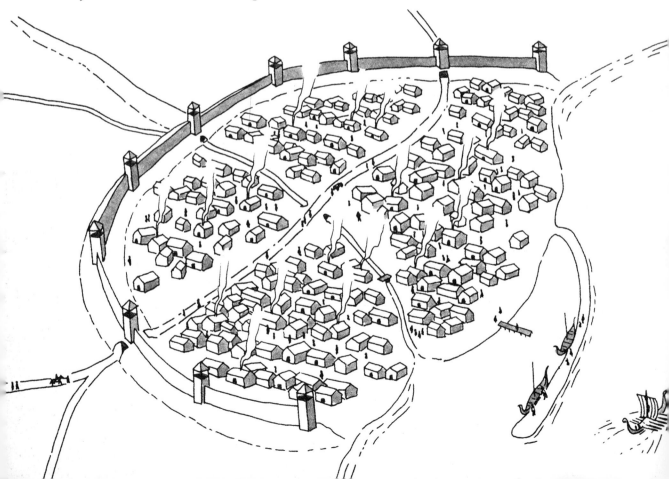

Houses

Viking buildings were very simple in style and houses normally consisted of just a single room. In the centre of the floor lay an open hearth with a hollowed-out roasting-pit. A hole in the roof above allowed smoke to escape but proper chimneys were unheard of. Along the sides of the room were drinking-benches and, at one end, the head of the household's High Seat. Occasionally, there were two additional rooms at the ends of the building: one used as sleeping quarters and the other to provide shelter for livestock.

The pictures show six different types of building. The simplest were constructed of either horizontal planks on a heavy timber framework (**a**), or else vertical staves (**b**). Wattle-and-daub houses were more popular (**c**).

Building materials had to be obtained locally. Where timber was unavailable or scarce, walls of stone were covered over with turf (**d**). This type was common in Viking settlements on the treeless islands of the North Atlantic Ocean.

On larger buildings, the heavy roof was supported by strong wooden posts both inside and around the outside (**e**). The **longhouse** (**f**) was also an example of this and often resembled an upturned boat in shape.

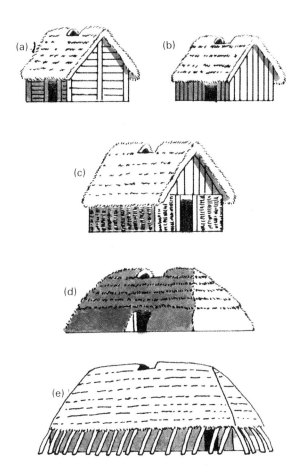

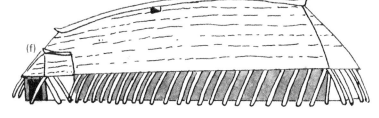

Personal cleanliness

Compared with most people living in Western Europe in the Dark Ages, the Scandinavians were a clean race. Most homes had a bath-house with a stone oven. The oven was heated until it was red hot, then splashed with cold water to make steam. This caused the bathers to sweat a lot, after which they cooled off by taking a plunge in a nearby stream.

The fastidiously clean Arabs, however, thought the Vikings to be 'the filthiest of God's creatures.' One writer, Ibn Fadlan, said:

Every morning a girl brings her master a bowl of water in which he washes his face, hands and hair . . . then blows his nose and spits into the water. (Then) the girl takes the same bowl to his neighbour who repeats the performance, until the bowl has gone round the entire household.

A pair of scales used by merchants to weigh out silver.

A collection of tenth-century Viking coins found in Dublin and York.

The Swordsmith's Art

The swordsmith was admired and respected above all other craftsmen. It took years for a man to learn the secrets of this art thoroughly, because of the tremendous skill involved.

The process began with the smelting of bog-ore in a **blast-furnace** to produce iron. The picture below shows a man working the bellows by hand to raise the temperature in the furnace.

To make a sword-blade strong and supple, the technique known as **pattern-welding** was used. First, several strips of iron were heated and twisted around one another. Then, while still hot, they were welded together by hammering.

Pattern-welded blades had a beautiful wavy grain along their surface, where the different strips had been intertwined. Some men said that this gave them the appearance of a snake coiled to strike and, thus, the legend of the magical, living sword was born.

A good swordsmith was always in great demand and many became rich and famous.

A swordsmith's workshop at Hedeby.

Things to do

Can You Remember?

1. Why was trading in Viking times such a risky business?
2. What were the qualities necessary to make a successful merchant?
3. Look at the maps on pages 66 and 67. What goods were obtained from England and the Byzantine Empire?
4. Name one area where furs were plentiful.
5. In what ways do you imagine the population of Hedeby differed from that of other parts of Scandinavia?
6. What materials did the Vikings build their homes from?
7. List the differences between buildings (**d**) and (**f**) on page 39.
8. Today, you can have a bath very similar to that taken by the Vikings. Where?
9. What exactly was smelting?
10. Describe the process known as 'pattern-welding'.

Activities

1. Using the maps on pages 66 and 67 as a guide, make a chart entitled *Viking Trade*. Use picture-symbols to represent the goods obtained from each country.
2. Draw a simple plan of Hedeby. Mark on it the rampart, roads and stream, also the mole around the harbour.
3. Make your own Viking coins from pieces of card, using the designs on page 40 to help you.

Group Project

Discuss in class why Hedeby was so well-placed to be an important trading-centre.

A small metal box for keeping scales in.

41

9 Vikings and the Law

For many Northmen, the most eventful time of year is midsummer when every freeborn man, whether simple farmer or noble chieftain, attends his local **Thing**, or Assembly.

All matters of importance are discussed at the Thing. Kings are proclaimed there; new laws are made and ancient ones upheld; disputes over hunting and pasture rights are settled and arguments between feuding families heard. Occasionally, such disputes are decided by *armed combat*. It is not unknown for a session to end with the marked-out battleground littered with corpses and whole families almost destroyed. Indeed, the assembled crowd looks forward to such *blood-lettings* since a good fight-to-the-death relieves the boredom of solemn oath-swearings and law-recitals.

Fairs are also held at the Thing. Traders come from Birka and Hedeby to sell iron goods, furs and salt; jugglers and acrobats amuse the gathering with their antics; poets tell stories of gods and battles, and feats of great strength are performed by the local champions. Occasionally, jarls and ships' captains send agents to the Thing to recruit

warriors for Viking expeditions overseas.

The *Thing-place* for the men of Skania is set on a prominent hill above the River Helge. It is clearly marked by a rune-stone erected beside a lonely thorn tree and is visible for miles around. Both stone and tree are very old and are held to be sacred. Each year, animals are sacrificed there, and their blood spilt on the ground around them.

At the first full moon after the heather has begun to bloom, Toke of Geirstad and his kinsmen fill their saddle-bags with food and jars of ale, and set off together on horseback to the Thing. Toke's elder sons, Orm and Grim, being promising young men, have also been allowed to go. Let us imagine the scene as the farmers gather round the *Thing-stone* to witness the proceedings.

Seated beside the stone is a snowy-haired old chieftain called Atli the Wise. For as long as men can remember, Atli has presided over the Thing as **Law-Speaker**. Now eighty years old, he can still recite all the laws by heart and his knowledge of customs and procedures is boundless.

The business dealt with this year promises to be very interesting. Two wealthy farmers, Stigand Sigtryggsson and Eyvind the Braggart, are involved in a **blood feud**. Both men are very powerful and influential in the area and keep armed retainers with them at all times. So far, thirty men have been killed in the course of the dispute. Twelve of them were burnt to death when Stigand set fire to Eyvind's longhouse. Each has accused the other of starting the feud and is claiming **wergeld**, or compensation, for the deaths of his kinsmen.

Among those whom Stigand has asked to swear an oath on his behalf is Toke of Geirstad. Though he would rather not be involved, Toke really has no choice since to refuse would bring revenge on his own family. In any case, Stigand is a great man in these parts and his support would be very useful should Toke himself ever be involved in a law-suit.

Viking Laws and Customs

Viking Scandinavia was a dangerous place for men to live alone. There were no police forces to uphold law and order and kings took little interest in their people except when it came to taxing them. It was a time when outlaws roamed the mountains and forests, and pirates raided villages along the coast. People lived together for safety. The members of the family, in particular, were expected to support each other against all dangers and attacks from without.

Laws were made to protect people's rights and property. They were not written but were passed down by word of mouth from one generation to the next. When the Thing was convened, it was the job of the Law-Speaker to recite all the laws from memory.

Legal disputes were not decided on the evidence presented but on the support each of the parties was able to muster up. Witnesses were called to swear oaths on behalf of either the accuser or the accused. They were not expected to have actually seen the crime but had just to testify, or swear to his innocence, whether they were sure of it or not. Naturally, a man's relatives would always testify on his behalf.

When the case was finally decided, the Assembly showed their agreement by a **wapentake**, or weapon-shaking.

Sometimes, trials were settled by **ordeal** or combat. In the case of the former, the accused had to carry a red-hot bar of iron for nine paces. If he let go of the bar before completing the ordeal, or if his hand did not heal within three days, he was found guilty. Trial-by-combat, or **holmgang**, often took place on small islands near the Thing-place or on areas specially marked out by four posts and a length of rope. Here, the accused and his accuser, or occasionally champions named by them, fought to the death.

Imprisonment was unknown as a punishment for free men. The death penalty was also rarely used. Thieves were hung only because it was thought they were bound to be too poor to repay their victims.

Murder and acts of violence were paid for by payments of **wergeld** to the victim or his family. The amount paid depended on the rank of the victim and the extent of his injuries. Jarls were entitled to half the wergeld of a king but twice that of a lesser chieftain. Ordinary freemen received the least of all. In each case, the full penalty was paid for murder or for chopping off a man's nose, half for poking out his eye, a quarter for his ear and so on.

In addition to any payment of compensation, the sentence of banishment or outlawry might also be imposed. Banishment meant leaving the country for three years; outlawry was for life. The person concerned was literally 'outside the law'. No man was allowed to provide him with food or shelter and anyone could kill him without fear of punishment.

Games and Pastimes

As one might expect of a warlike people, the Vikings were very fond of violent sports and games. Wrestling was extremely popular and took place on dry land or in deep water. In the latter case, the object was to hold one's opponent beneath the surface until he gave in. Local strongmen also took part in boulder-lifting and caber-tossing.

King Olaf Tryggvason was a renowned athlete. According to the sagas he could:

> run across the oars of the *Serpent* (his longship) while his men were rowing the vessel. He could juggle with three daggers so that one was always in the air, and he caught the one falling by the handle. He could walk all round the ship's gunwales, could strike and cut equally well with both hands, and could throw two spears at once.

We hear that King Olaf was also an accomplished mountaineer.

Horse-fighting had an enthusiastic following (see page 19) and often caused brawls between the owners and their supporters which ended in blood-feuds.

Quieter forms of relaxation included board games such as **Fox and Geese**. The object here was that one piece in the centre, representing the fox, should avoid being driven into a corner by ten or twelve geese. It is thought that Viking merchants also brought the game of chess with them to Northern Europe from the East. The boards themselves were often fitted with specially bored holes and pegged pieces so that games could be played on ships in rough seas.

Stigand is Banished

The oaths having been sworn, the time has now come to decide the case between Stigand Sigtryggsson and Eyvind the Braggart. Atli the Wise rises from his chair to address the Assembly. He suggests that both parties should pay wergeld to the dead men's kinsfolk. In addition, Stigand, who burnt down Eyvind's longhouse, should be placed under banishment. The Thing-men show their agreement by shouting and rattling their swords, making a terrific din.

In this way the Thing of Skania is brought to a close. The men pull down their tents and make ready for the journey home. Before they leave, Stigand Sigtryggsson announces to the company that he is to go a-Viking and has room for three ships' crews to accompany him. He has heard that Thorkel the Tall is to lead a great expedition to the West and that vast riches await anyone who cares to join him. Many of the younger men present eagerly voice their intention to come along, among them Grim Tokesson. For a long time now, Grim has been restless to follow his sword across the sea. Few prospects await younger sons here at home while abroad lies the chance of land, gold and adventure.

Wrestling was a popular sport.

Things to do

Can You Remember?

1. Mention three types of business dealt with at the Thing.
2. What would we call such an assembly today?
3. What other activities also took place during the meeting of the Thing?
4. Why was law enforcement so difficult in Viking Scandinavia?
5. Why was the job of Law-Speaker so important?
6. What was 'oath-swearing'?
7. Describe trial by ordeal and combat.
8. What was wergeld? How was the amount to be paid assessed?
9. Apart from paying wergeld to their victims, how else could wrongdoers be punished?
10. In the north of England, local assemblies came to be known as 'wapentakes'. Where does this word come from?

Activities

1. In your opinion, how fair and reliable was the Vikings' system of justice?
2. Make an illustrated chart entitled *Viking Games and Pastimes*.
3. Design and make the face of a rune-stone. The characters of the runic alphabet are on page 11.

Group Project

Write a play about a legal dispute being settled at the Thing. Members of the class can perform the various parts.

10 Hammer and Raven

Like all his neighbours, Toke Gudbrandsson is a heathen. For generations, he and his ancestors have worshipped the ancient gods of the North. The Vikings look to these to give them protection in times of war and peace: protection against enemies who would do them harm, and against famine and disease. The gods, however, are a fickle bunch. Despite all the sacrifices offered up to them, they might still choose to send ships to the bottom of the sea, or to grant victory in battle to one's opponent. But despite this fickleness, the simple farmers continue to serve them.

But times are now changing in the North. Thirty years ago, shaven-headed priests from Saxony and England journeyed to Denmark to spread tales of a new God, the White Christ. They said that men should renounce their false idols, who were surely sons of the Devil, and that they should forgive their enemies, loving one another as brothers.

The shaven priests were so successful that none other than the late Harald Bluetooth, King of the Danes, allowed himself to be converted to the new religion. Many of his people followed suit and, soon, small churches began to appear above field and meadow.

47

The Old Gods

Meanwhile in the far-flung reaches of the kingdom, the old customs linger on. In Skania, the shaven men were at first treated with scorn and suspicion, later with outright hostility. The people of these parts resented the attacks made on their gods and handed the newcomers over to their own priests for sacrifice.

Others, of a more business-like nature, hung chains on them and sold them at a healthy profit to the wild forest-folk inland.

Here, **Odin** and **Thor** continue to reign supreme and, each year, animals and humans alike are slaughtered in dark oak groves in order to satisfy the gods' thirst for blood.

The World of the Gods

Asgard

Jotunheim

Bifrost

Midgard

Hel

The Vikings' World of Gods and Men

The Vikings believed in a supernatural world of gods, giants, trolls and dragons. The gods lived in a beautiful city in the sky called **Asgard** which could be reached from Earth by crossing the rainbow-bridge, **Bifrost**. Further away was **Jotunheim**, a mountainous waste-land inhabited by giants who were the enemies of the gods. Beneath everything lay the dark and gloomy underworld called **Hel**, land of the dead.

This state of affairs was not to last forever. At the end of the world, or **Ragnarök**, the gods and giants would fight one last, great battle. Then, everything would be destroyed and the world would be consumed by fire.

The Norse Gods

Odin was the god of battles, poetry and wisdom. He was a mighty warlord and had an eight-legged horse, **Sleipnir**. Two ferocious wolves stood on either side of him while two ravens sat on his shoulders and brought him news of what was happening in the world. Odin had female servants called **Valkyries** who rode down to the battlefields on Earth, choosing slain warriors to bring back with them to Asgard. There, the dead heroes fought and feasted in Odin's Great Hall, **Valhalla**, waiting to follow him to battle with the giants at Ragnarök.

Thor was the god of thunder and lightning and was most popular with ordinary farmers who looked to him to give them good weather for their crops. He was a huge, powerful,

red-bearded god who, though kind and jovial, had a fierce temper. Thor rode through the sky in a chariot pulled by goats and wielded a magic hammer, **Mjollnir**, which made the sound of thunder whenever he threw it.

There was also **Tyr**, like Odin, a god of war, **Frey**, the god of fertility and **Freyja**, the goddess of love.

Most mischievous of the gods was **Loki**. He was always on the lookout to cause trouble and misery to his fellows yet, when they tried to gain their revenge, he usually managed to escape their clutches. When they finally caught him, they bound him to a rock beneath the dripping jaws of a venomous serpent. Loki's wife held out a bowl to catch the poison but when she turned away to empty it, a few drops fell on his face, causing him to writhe in agony. This writhing shook the mountains and was the cause of earthquakes.

Loki had three terrible children: the **Midgard Serpent** which coiled itself around the Earth; the fierce and enormous **Fenris Wolf**; and **Hela**, guardian of the underworld where people not fortunate enough to be killed in battle were sent.

49

Religious and burial customs

The Vikings' religious festivals were often bloodthirsty affairs. The German historian, Adam of Bremen, once described their most famous pagan temple at Old Uppsala in Sweden:

> In this temple, completely covered with gold, are three idols which the Swedes worship: Thor, the mightiest god, has his throne in the middle of the hall, and Odin and Frey are on either side of him.
>
> Attached to the gods are priests who offer up sacrifices. If disease or famine threaten they sacrifice to the idol Thor; if there is war, to Odin; and if a wedding is to be celebrated they sacrifice to Frey.

Adam went on to describe the Nine Year Festival at Uppsala which everyone was forced to attend by law:

> The sacrifice at this event involves the slaughter of nine males of every creature, with whose blood the gods are pacified. The bodies are hung in a grove near the temple. . . . Dogs and horses hang there beside human beings, and a Christian has told me that he has seen up to seventy-two corpses hanging there side by side.

As part of their heathen religion, the Vikings believed in another world to which they passed after death. For that reason, they were buried or cremated with any possessions which they might need during the journey to this next 'life'.

Ordinary people were buried in simple graves dressed in their finest clothes together with their weapons and items of food and drink. Sometimes, the grave was marked by stones being placed over it in the form of a ship.

The bodies of kings and chieftains were laid out on board their longships which were dragged ashore and either burnt in a funeral-pyre or buried intact under a great mound of earth. Occasionally, their wives and servants were taken to the next world with them.

The Coming of Christianity

From the start of the Viking Age, Christian missionaries travelled to Scandinavia in order to persuade the Northmen to give up their pagan beliefs. In doing so, they risked their lives and, indeed, many were martyred in the cause of the God they called the White Christ.

Following the conversion of the Danish King Harald Bluetooth in the late tenth century, Christianity became more widely accepted in the North. Some Vikings were forced to adopt the new religion at the point of a sword, but most simply came to accept that the loving and forgiving Christ offered them more hope than the old untrustworthy gods of Asgard.

The following extract from **Heimskringla** describes the efforts of King Olaf Tryggvason of Norway and his missionaries to spread the new religion to Iceland:

The sacrificial groves at Old Uppsala.

Thangbrand the Priest returned to King Olaf from Iceland with stories of his fruitless efforts, complaining that the Icelanders had composed rude poems about him, that some had even tried to kill him and that there was little hope of the country ever becoming Christian.

King Olaf was so angry at this that he ordered all of the Icelanders then living in the town to be brought to him for execution. But Kjartan, Gizur and Hjalte, and other Icelanders who had been baptised went to him and said, 'King . . . however much any man might annoy you, you must forgive him if he turns from paganism and becomes a Christian; and with their help we might then bring Christianity to Iceland, because many of them are the sons of Iceland's greatest families and have great influence. But Thangbrand, on the other hand, carried out his business with violence and manslaughter, and the people there would not submit to this kind of behaviour.'

According to the writer, the King was swayed by this speech and soon afterwards, as a result of the Icelanders' sensible advice, their country was peacefully converted to Christianity.

Scene from a Gotland picture-stone: Odin mounted on his eight-legged steed, Sleipnir.

Things to do

Can You Remember?
1. What is a pagan or heathen?
2. Where were the Norse gods supposed to live?
3. Which gods were symbolised by the hammer and raven?
4. Which gods do you imagine were worshipped by:
   (a) kings and chieftains?
   (b) farmers?
   (c) people about to marry?
5. One of the gods had no worshippers. Which one?
6. What was to happen on the day of Ragnarök?
7. Four of our days of the week are named after Viking gods. What are they?
8. What do you think was a Viking's ultimate ambition?
9. Why were people buried with their most valued possessions?
10. Explain how the Northmen were eventually converted to Christianity.

Activities
1. Look in an atlas for places in England which are named after Odin or Thor (the Anglo-Saxons called Odin, *Woden*). Why were these places given such names?
2. Draw up a list of items which a Viking chieftain might want to take with him to the next world.
3. Describe an imaginary conversation between a heathen Viking and a Christian missionary. Compare the two religions.

Group Project
Read more about the Viking gods in a book on Norse myths and legends.

11 Ships and Seafarers

As a result of his banishment, Stigand Sigtryggsson is to join Thorkel the Tall's forthcoming expedition to the West. Many others have come forward to serve in his crew, so many, in fact, that he has had to have a new longship built in addition to the three he has already.

The most famous shipwright in Skania is a man called Aslak Holmskalle. He has practised his craft for almost forty years and owns a shipyard down on the coast, where he has many men working for him. Some are freemen: skilled carpenters who cut and shape the timber, and blacksmiths who make the metal fittings. Others are thralls. They do the heavy work of carrying tree-trunks and logs, or messy jobs like applying tar to the ship's hull.

After much haggling, Aslak has agreed to build Stigand's ship at short notice for six hundred pieces of silver. This is as much as Stigand can afford and he has had to sell his farm to meet the cost.

Since a Viking's most precious possession is his ship, ship-building is a serious affair. Prayers are sent up to the gods before each plank is cut or planed and all the rules are correctly observed in the vessel's construction.

The Viking Ship

Without the ship, there would have been no Viking Age. It was the development of these beautifully designed boats which made it possible for Scandinavians to brave the rough northern seas in search of other lands to conquer and settle in.

There were two basic designs: the man-of-war commonly called the **longship**, and the shorter, more heavily built **knorr** or merchant ship. Both had open decks and were propelled by a single, square sail and two rows of oars. There was also a large steering-oar at the **stern** on the **starboard** side. Viking ships were **clinker-built** which means that the planks running along both sides overlapped one another in order to make the vessel stronger and more watertight.

As one might expect, Viking captains were immensely proud of their ships and gave them special names, like *Long Serpent*, *Bison* and *Sea Raven*. They also painted, or gilded, the dragon head on the prow and hung richly decorated shields over the **gunwales** (pronounced *gunnels*).

The following verses from **Heimskringla** describe a Norwegian fleet setting off to do battle with the Danes. A crowd of womenfolk and girls are watching from the quayside as the ships embark:

The Oseberg ship's ornamental prow: Viking craftsmanship at its best.

The dragon-head of a Swedish longship.

My pretty girl! the sight was grand
When the great longship down the strand
Into the river gently slid
And all below her sides was hid
Come, pretty girls, and see the show!
Her sides that on the water glow,
Her serpent-head with golden mane,
All shining back from the Nid again.

It was upon a Saturday,
Ship-tilts were struck and stowed away,
And past the town our dragon glides,
That girls might see our glancing sides.
Out from the Nid brave Harald steers;
Westward at first the dragon veers;
Our lads together down with oars,
The splash is echoed round the shores.

Their oars the King's men handle well,
One stroke is all the eye can tell:
All level over the water rise;
The girls look on in sheer surprise.
Such things, they think, can ne'er give way;
They little know the battle-day
The Danish girls, who dread our shout,
Might wish our ship-gear not so stout.

trans. S. Laing

53

Felling and preparing the timber

Even when not actually engaged in constructing a vessel, a shipwright would roam the forests nearby, searching for timber suitable for his task. Oak was the most popular material to use on account of its size and strength but was becoming scarce in parts of Scandinavia due to over use. Other types of timber had to be used occasionally, such as pine, ash and birch, but the **keel** (the backbone of the ship) was always made from oak. Tall, straight trees were selected for the keel and planking while those with a natural bend in the grain were used for curved parts such as the ribs.

Winter was the normal season for felling timber since the sapless trees were easier to cut. When the trees were cut down, they were stored, possibly for several years, at the bottom of lakes to prevent them from rotting and to make the timber more supple. They were later taken out and stored so that they could dry slowly without cracking.

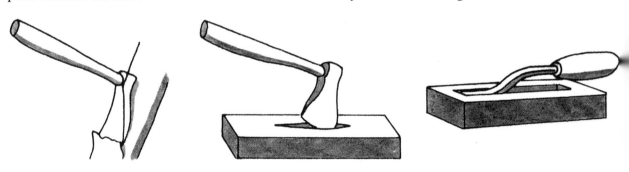

adze for shaping cut wood   **axe for cutting planks**   **chisel for cutting grooves in wood**

Building a longship

Viking shipwrights were superb craftsmen. Each *rib*, *plank* and *strake* was fashioned by eye and rule of thumb, yet fitted exactly into place. The keel and outer skin were built first, then fastened to the ribs and cross-beams with tough cord to give the vessel the flexibility needed to ride the towering waves of the North Atlantic.

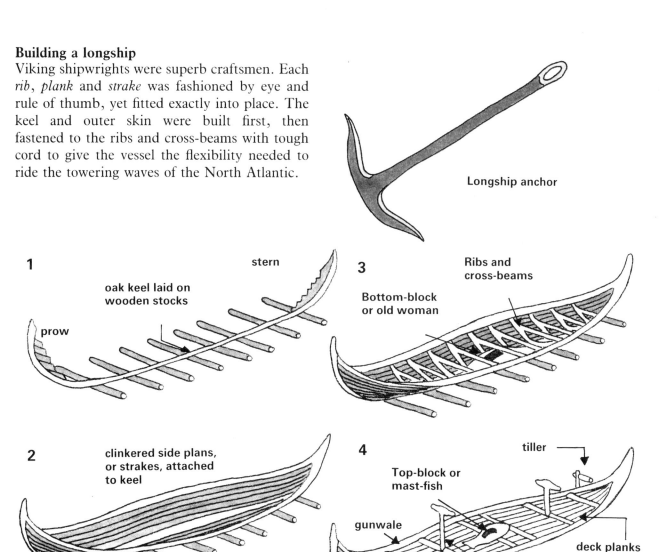

Longship anchor

1
stern
oak keel laid on wooden stocks
prow

2
clinkered side plans, or strakes, attached to keel
gaps between strakes plugged with tar and rope

3
Ribs and cross-beams
Bottom-block or old woman

4
tiller
Top-block or mast-fish
gunwale
deck planks
trestle on which to rest mast and oars when not in use

Life at sea

Life on board a Viking longship was extremely uncomfortable. Except for an awning which could be rigged above the deck, there was no shelter from the elements and much of a voyage was spent baling out water which had spilled over the gunwales.

Enough food and fresh water was taken on board to last the crew several days. When they ran out, the warriors would engage in a **strandhogg**. That is, they robbed farms on the coast of their livestock, barbecuing their stolen gains on the beach before setting off again.

Helmsmen steered close to land as far as possible, making a note of landmarks such as cliffs and estuaries. For travelling across open sea, they were guided by the position of the sun and stars.

Stigand's Voyage

By midsummer, Stigand Sigtryggsson's new longship is ready for service. He is well-pleased with the results of Aslak's work. The vessel is low and sleek with a shallow draught: excellent for quick acceleration and for penetrating shallow waters. There are fifteen pairs of oars and a fierce-looking dragon head on the **prow**. A huge square sail with red and white stripes hangs from the mast.

Such a fine ship ought to have a name. Stigand decides to name it after himself. Everyone thinks this an excellent choice since the name, *Stigand*, in the Norse language, means 'Strider': in other words, a ship which 'hauls the sea under it quickly'.

Throughout the North, warriors have answered the call to Thorkel the Tall's banner, fired by stories of the rich plunder to be found in England and the West. Some, like Stigand Sigtryggsson, are outlaws, banished from their native land. They mean to satisfy their appetites for violence on the poor inhabitants of countries overseas. Many more are landless young men who hope to find greener pastures abroad on which to raise their herds. Others simply find the quiet life at home boring and long to follow the whale's path in search of fame and fortune.

England is renowned for the wealth of its towns and monasteries. For twenty years now, King Ethelred the Redeless (the Ill-Advised) has been generous to the men of the North since, instead of sending out armies to chase them away, he pays them large amounts of silver, or **Danegeld** to leave his shores.

Among the crew of the *Stigand* is Grim Tokesson. This will be his first Viking cruise and his father has given him an iron helmet, a studded leather jerkin and a beautifully carved broad-axe. Toke, himself, wielded this same axe when he, as a young man, went on his adventures abroad. He tells his son to be ever watchful and to carry his weapons with him at all times if he wishes to see old age.

On the day *Stigand* is due to set sail, the crews' families line the shore to say farewell to their menfolk. It is an emotional time. Wives and mothers know that they may never see their loved ones again. Then who will be left to farm the land or keep the wolf from the door?

But the warriors are eager to be off. They load the longships with enough provisions to see them through the voyage ahead: casks of ale and water, tubs of salted meat and smoked fish, butter and cheese and sacks of grain. When their cloaks and weapons are on board the cramped decks, there is little room left for the men. At last, when all is ready, the oars are lowered and the longships rowed out towards the sea. Friends and families wave from the jetty until the ships are mere dots on the horizon.

Detail from the Bayeux Tapestry

The raiders sail West over the sea.

Things to do

Can You Remember?

1. What was the difference between a longship and a knorr?
2. Explain what is meant by the expression 'clinker-built'.
3. Why was oak the most suitable material for shipbuilding?
4. How was the wood preserved?
5. What was the most important part of the ship's structure?
6. Where do you think the nautical term starboard came from?
7. Why was it so important for a Viking longship to have a shallow draught?
8. Give two circumstances under which the oars would be necessary to propel the ship.
9. What was a 'strandhogg'?
10. How did Viking crews navigate their ships across the sea?

Activities

1. Look at the maps on pages 66 and 67. Remember also what conditions were like in Scandinavia. Why were ships so important to the Vikings?
2. Draw and label a picture of a longship.
3. Write a 'log' for a Viking voyage lasting seven days.

Group Project

Make a frieze for your classroom wall showing a fleet of Viking longships.

A Viking fleet carved on a piece of wood.

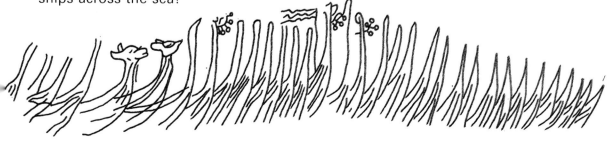

12 King Ethelred's Kingdom

It is almost three years now since Thorkel the Tall's great Viking fleet set sail for the West. Never before had such a splendid and well-equipped host left the shores of Denmark: fifty-five ships, each with towering mast and gilded dragon's head, and three thousand of the most formidable warriors to be found in the northern countries.

Having set sail with a clear sky and a strong wind behind, the longships rounded the Skaw and proceeded down the North Sea coast towards the flat wastes of Friesland. Then, after several weeks plundering Frisian villages, the fleet made for the Kentish coast of England. The men from these parts had no wish to battle with such a large army of seasoned warriors. Instead they paid the invaders 3,000 pounds of silver to sail away.

The Vikings spent the first winter on an island in the Thames estuary before making a blistering attack on London early the following year. But the town's inhabitants fought back so strongly that the Danes were forced to withdraw to their camp.

In the spring, the fleet sailed up the coast to Ipswich, sacked the town and went raiding in East Anglia. The chieftain of the East Angles was a mighty warrior called Ulfkell Snilling. He had fought against the Danes before and there were many in Thorkel's army who remembered the hard sword-play Ulfkell had given them.

The Vikings fell upon the English at a desolate place called Ringmere Heath. There, a fierce and bloody battle was fought, with many killed on either side. At first, the Danish onslaught was repeatedly repulsed by the brave English, standing firm in their **shield-ring** and urged on by Ulfkell. But Jarl Thorkel and his mail-clad housecarls eventually broke through the enemy ranks, cutting great swathes in front of them with axe and sword so that, in the end, the Vikings had the victory.

Far from their ships, on Ringmere plain,
In heaps your warriors pile the slain;
This tale, O King, I understood:
That Ringmere Heath ran red with blood.
In battle where the shields resound,
The Englishmen crash to the ground;
They bow before you in the fight,
And many more are killed in flight.

The whole country now lay defenceless before the invading army. For eighteen months, they travelled the land, burning towns and plundering abbeys, maiming and murdering wherever they went. The end came when, after the Danes had attacked Canterbury and murdered Archbishop Alphege, King Ethelred was finally forced to dig inside his coffers once again and bribe the Danes with 48,000 pounds of silver to leave his kingdom in peace.

A grisly relic

It is said that the English, whenever they managed to catch a Viking in the act of looting their village, would flay him alive and nail his skin to the church door. The picture shows a fragment of human skin taken from the door of Hadstock Church in Essex.

The payment of Danegeld

Danegeld was the money paid by European monarchs to persuade invading Viking armies to go away. Naturally enough, they nearly always came back for more. A Swedish runestone tells of a certain Ulf who:

> has in England taken three gelds. That was the first which Toste paid. Then Thorkel paid. Then Canute paid.

Huge hoards of silver coins, many of them English in origin, have been found in Scandinavia.

Viking England

The first raids on England were recorded in the late eighth century but it was not for another eighty years that the Vikings actually came to settle. In A.D.876, Halfdan shared out the lands of Northumbria among his followers and, for a while, it looked as though the Vikings would conquer the whole of England. But King Alfred the Great defeated them in battle and a boundary was drawn between English territory in the South-West and the **Danelaw** in the North-East.

After a period of relative peace, the raids began again during the disastrous reign of King Ethelred the Redeless and, between A.D.1014 and A.D.1042, England was ruled by Danish Kings.

The last Viking invasion took place in A.D.1066 when King Harald Hardrada of Norway was killed at the battle at Stamford Bridge, just a month before William of Normandy's victory at Hastings.

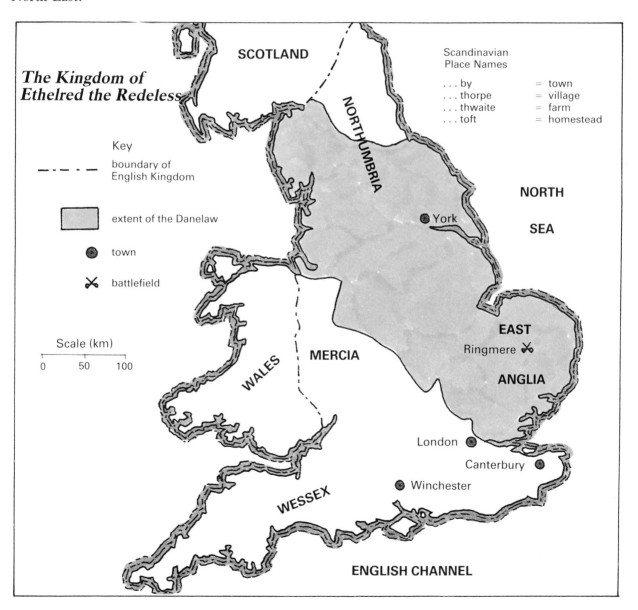

The Kingdom of Ethelred the Redeless

SCOTLAND

Scandinavian Place Names

. . . by	= town
. . . thorpe	= village
. . . thwaite	= farm
. . . toft	= homestead

Key

– · – · – boundary of English Kingdom

extent of the Danelaw

● town

✂ battlefield

Scale (km)
0   50   100

NORTHUMBRIA

● York

NORTH SEA

WALES

MERCIA

EAST ANGLIA

Ringmere ✂

London ●

Canterbury ●

● Winchester

WESSEX

ENGLISH CHANNEL

Our Viking heritage

The Viking influence is most clearly seen in Northern England where many of the place-names are of Scandinavian origin, as well as towns such as Derby, Scunthorpe and Lowestoft.

The Norse language has also given us words such as: *awkward, bank, birth, booth, brink, both, bull, calf, call, crawl, cut, die, drown, egg, fellow, happy, husband, husting, ill, kid, knife, law, leg, lift, loose, odd, race, reef, riding, rift, scare, seemly, sister, skin, skull, take, their, them, they, thrift, trust, ugly, want, weak* and *wrong*.

Possibly the most lasting legacy left to us by the Vikings was their legal system, with the holding of **Things**, called **wapentakes** (see page 44), to settle disputes. It was the Danish custom to swear in juries of twelve freemen for the purpose of trying such cases, a procedure unknown before in England.

A Viking rune-stone found in St. Paul's Churchyard, London.

The Warriors Return

The Danegeld has at last been collected and Thorkel the Tall's army paid off by its English hosts. After the spoils of war have been duly divided, the warriors prepare to depart.

Stigand Sigtryggsson is well-satisfied with his good fortune. His men have plundered far and wide, capturing large quantities of silver plate and jewellery,

The Yttergärde Stone in Uppland, Sweden, telling of Ulf's three payments of geld.

so that his longships lie low under the weight of all the booty he has taken. He will return home a wealthy and honoured man and now that his three years of banishment are up, he is ready to resume, with renewed vigour, his old feud with Eyvind the Braggart.

Not all of the Vikings will be leaving with him, however. None other than Thorkel the Tall himself has agreed to enter the service of King Ethelred as a hired mercenary, helping to defend his kingdom against other foreigners hungry for land and gold. For this, he will be well paid, and any other man who wishes to join him.

Grim Tokesson has decided to follow Jarl Thorkel. He lost his share of the Danegeld when he became drunk one night and had his hard-earned silver stolen by a young English girl he had taken into his tent with him. A Viking who returns home penniless is held in low esteem by his fellows when others have fared so well.

Receiving Danegeld.

Things to do

Can You Remember?

1. Why did the Vikings find England such a profitable country to raid?
2. For what other reason did they come here?
3. In what way was Ethelred the Redeless considered to be a weak king?
4. What was Danegeld?
5. How many gelds did the Swede, Ulf, receive?
6. The Vikings carried a banner into battle with the figure of a raven emblazoned upon it. What do you think was the raven's significance?
7. How did the English often deal with Viking raiders who fell into their hands?
8. Where in England did the Danes mostly settle?
9. How do you think the Danelaw received its name?
10. Mention two things which the Vikings have passed down to us.

Activities

1. Trace the map on page 61. Mark the route followed by Jarl Thorkel's expedition.
2. Write a story about the battle at Ringmere Heath.
3. Find a book on English Christian and surnames. How many pupils in your class have names of Scandinavian origin?

Group Project

Draw a large-scale map of England, mounted on a piece of hardboard. Using different-coloured drawing pins, mark on towns and villages with Scandinavian name-endings. See how closely their distribution corresponds to the extent of the Danelaw.

13 Vikings East and West

In the last chapter, you learned about the Vikings in England. In fact, this country was just one of many to feel the effects, both brutal and otherwise, of the Northmen. Their ships' prows ranged from the Arctic Ocean in the North to the Mediterranean in the South; from the Caspian Sea in the East to the inhospitable islands of the North Atlantic in the West.

The **Danes** attacked England, France and Friesland, while those more daring sailed as far as Moorish Spain, passing through the **Njörva Sound** (Straits of Gibraltar) to raid along the coast of Italy. Danish settlements sprang up on either side of the North Sea and the King of the Franks was forced to give them a part of his kingdom, today called Normandy.

Driven from their lands by powerful kings, the **Norwegians** came to settle in Scotland and Ireland, and even sailed across the ocean to found colonies in Iceland and Greenland. A few shiploads, at least, got as far as North America, called **Vinland**.

The Baltic Sea and the East was the **Swedes'** domain. They penetrated the vast forests and steppes of what is today Russia, carrying their boats from river to river, all the way to Constantinople, which they called **Miklagrad**, or the 'Great City'.

The Vikings in France

Throughout the ninth century, France suffered terribly at the hands of the Vikings. With the country frequently in a state of civil war and navigable rivers penetrating far inland, raiding was an easy business. Paris was sacked on several occasions and many Danegelds paid.

Then in A.D.911, King Charles the Simple granted territory in the North to the Viking, Rollo, to protect his coast against other pirates. According to one chronicler:

> When the time came for Rollo to be created Duke . . . the bishops said to him, 'When you receive the honour, you must kneel and kiss the King's foot.' Rollo replied, 'I have never bowed before any man, let alone kiss his foot.' Finally, he gave way to the pleadings of the Franks and commanded one of his men to kiss the King's foot. The Northman bent down and, seizing the royal foot, stood up to kiss it, throwing the King on his back amidst the roars of laughter from the assembled crowd.

These Northmen, or **Normans**, as they came to be called, rapidly settled down, becoming Christians, adopting French customs and inter-marrying with the native population. They learned to build great castles, cathedrals and churches from stone, and enforced strong laws to protect people. They copied more advanced methods of warfare, fighting as armed knights on horseback.

Their leaders became mighty conquerors. Some travelled South to Sicily and founded a kingdom there. In A.D.1066, Duke William of Normandy defeated the English King Harold at the Battle of Hastings and took his crown.

River routes to the East

Adventurers from Sweden sailed across the Baltic Sea to conquer the wild Slavs of Eastern Europe. They also came as merchants, navigating the great rivers Volga, Dnieper and Dvina which, as a result, became important trade-routes between East and West.

The journey to Constantinople was full of danger. Fierce tribes of horsemen, Bulgars and Patzinaks, lurked along the river-routes, and plunging rapids threatened to wreck many a ship. The following extract explains how the **Rus** (as the Vikings in the East were known) dealt with these hazards:

> (At the fourth set of rapids), the **Rus** turn their ships' prows into the bank and run them aground. They then send a company of guards into the surrounding countryside to look out for the Patzinaks, their enemies, who are always waiting to ambush them. They unload the ships and march their slaves in chains across land for six miles. The boats are then lifted out of the water and half carried, half dragged overland. Once past the rapids, they lower them once more into the water, load them with their goods and sail off again.

The Rus founded two powerful states at Novgorod and Kiev. For a while they even challenged the might of the Byzantine Empire.

In A.D.907, their leader, Oleg, arrived at Constantinople with two thousand ships, but the Greeks fortified the strait (narrow channel) and put a chain across the Bosphorus. Oleg landed and commanded his men to ground their ships. They pillaged the countryside around the city and killed many Greeks. Of the prisoners they captured, some were beheaded, some tortured and some cast into the sea.

As time went by, the Rus began to get on better with the Byzantines. Some of them even joined the Emperor's bodyguard, called the **Varangian Guard**, performing legendary feats of daring and courage. Even rulers like King Harald Hardrada of Norway were proud to have fought in its ranks.

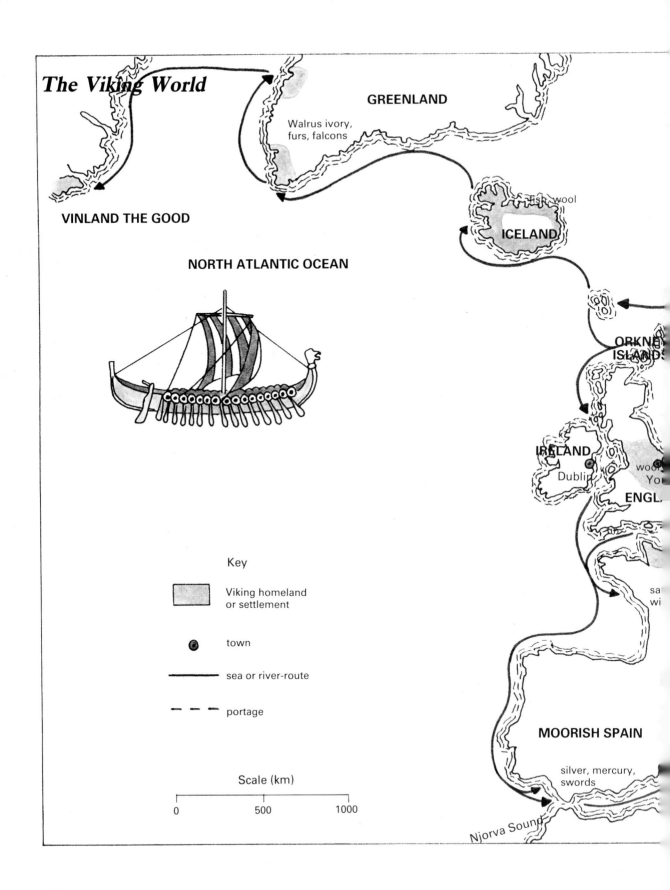

The Viking World

GREENLAND

Walrus ivory, furs, falcons

VINLAND THE GOOD

ICELAND

fish, wool

NORTH ATLANTIC OCEAN

ORKNEY ISLANDS

IRELAND

Dublin

wool

York

ENGLAND

Key

Viking homeland or settlement

town

sea or river-route

portage

salt wine

MOORISH SPAIN

silver, mercury, swords

Scale (km)

0   500   1000

Njorva Sound

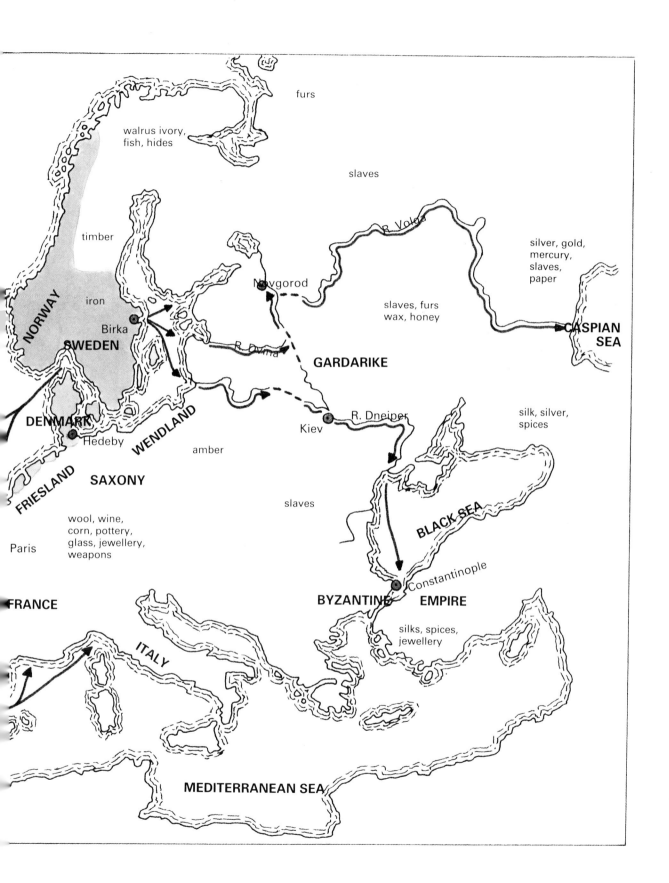

furs

walrus ivory,
fish, hides

slaves

NORWAY

timber

iron

R. Volga

silver, gold,
mercury,
slaves,
paper

Birka

SWEDEN

Novgorod

GARDARIKE

slaves, furs
wax, honey

CASPIAN
SEA

R. Dvina

DENMARK

WENDLAND

Hedeby

FRIESLAND

SAXONY

amber

Kiev

R. Dneiper

silk, silver,
spices

slaves

BLACK SEA

Paris

wool, wine,
corn, pottery,
glass, jewellery,
weapons

FRANCE

ITALY

BYZANTINE

Constantinople

EMPIRE

silks, spices,
jewellery

MEDITERRANEAN SEA

Explorers of the North Atlantic

The Vikings' most daring voyages were made across the northern seas. They came first to Iceland, volcanic and treeless, yet swiftly colonised the island and settled down as sheep farmers. Away from the tyranny of kings, they set up their own parliament, or **Althing**, which still exists today.

One Icelander, Erik the Red, was outlawed for killing some men and sailed further West. He discovered a cold, mountainous land which he called Greenland, rather dishonestly, to attract other settlers.

They built their homes above the lake; some of their houses were near the waterside, and others farther away. They spent the winter there. No snow fell and all of their livestock were able to graze.

Unfortunately, the colony was not to last:

> Then early one morning, they looked about them and saw a number of skin-canoes being paddled up from the South. . . . They were dark, ugly men who wore their hair in a strange fashion. They had large eyes and broad cheekbones.

At first, the **Skraelings**, as these primitive natives were called, traded peacefully with the newcomers. But later, relations worsened and they made several attacks on the settlement. They were beaten off each time but their very presence, and the Vikings' lack of numbers, meant that it was no longer safe to stay. It would be another five hundred years before this land would be rediscovered.

Erik's son, Leif, had heard tales of yet another land to the West. In the year 1000, he made an epic voyage, sailing past rocky coasts and icebergs until he reached a land so warm and pleasant that grapes were found growing on the trees. Leif Eriksson named it **Vinland**, or 'wine-land'.

More Vikings ventured there bringing their families with them. According to the Saga of Erik the Red:

> That spring, Karlsefni and his men sailed a long way down the coast until they came to a river. . . . Ashore they found fields of natural corn . . . and vines wherever there were woods. Every stream was full of fish. . . .

The End of the Viking Age

The Viking period of mayhem and destruction lasted for over 250 years. In that time they made a tremendous impact on the lives of their European neighbours who, in turn, gradually succeeded in civilising the wild men of the North. The invaders, who at first came to rob and kill, eventually settled down, exchanging their swords for ploughs. In time, they became almost indistinguishable from the native population, speaking their language and obeying their laws.

Most importantly, the Vikings became Christians. Their fierce, old woodland gods lived on only in poems and sagas, especially in Iceland where they were written down and can still be read today.

Back in their homelands in Scandinavia, kings strengthened their hold over their subjects, appointing royal officials to administer their realms and collect taxes. Such kings had little love for the old independent type of sea-rover, keeping his war-band around him and going off to raid other lands, causing friction with their rulers.

Soon, the sight of brightly painted warships, with their dragons' heads and rows of shields hung over the gunwales, became a thing of the past. The Northmen continued to follow the prow, not as pirates but as peaceful traders. The Age of the Vikings was over.

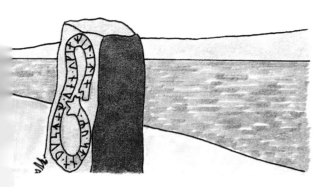

One thing will never die — the reputation a man leaves behind him.

Things to do

Can You Remember?

1. Give two reasons why it was easy for the Danes to attack France?
2. How did Normandy get its name?
3. Why did the King of the Franks grant land to the Vikings?
4. Who were the Rus?
5. How did the Swedes get their ships all the way from the Baltic to the Black Sea?
6. Why did Vikings from Norway seek new lands?
7. What was the Althing?
8. Why did Leif Eriksson call his new land, Vinland?
9. What place had he, in fact, discovered?
10. Who do you think were the Skraelings?

Activities

1. Look at the maps on pages 66 and 67. Where, respectively, did the Danes, Norwegians and Swedes operate?
2. Imagine that you were a Viking settler in Vinland. Describe your first winter there.
3. Make a time-chart, giving the main dates of the Viking Age. Look back at other chapters in this book for your information.

Group Project

How have we been able to obtain so much information about the Vikings? What archaeological and written sources do we have?

Glossary/Index

Books to Read

(Some of these titles may no longer be available in bookshops but they would be worth asking for in the library.)

GENERAL HISTORIES

J. Brøndsted, **The Vikings**, Penguin, 1960.

G. Jones, **A History of the Vikings**, Oxford, 1968.

R. R. Sellman, **The Vikings**, Methuen, 1957.

J. Simpson, **Everyday Life in the Viking Age**, Batsford, 1967.

SAGAS, MYTHS AND LEGENDS

Egil's Saga (Trans. C. Fell), Dent, 1975

R. L. Green, **The Myths of the Norsemen**, Penguin, 1960.

G. Jones, **Scandinavian Myths and Legends**, Oxford, 1956

King Harald's Saga (Trans. M. Magnusson and H. Palsson), Penguin, 1966.

Laxdaela Saga (Trans. M. Magnusson and H. Palsson), Penguin, 1969.

Njal's Saga (Trans. M. Magnusson and H. Palsson), Penguin, 1960.

The Vinland Sagas (Trans. M. Magnusson and H. Palsson), Penguin, 1965.

NOVELS

F. Bengtsson, **The Long Ships**, Collins, 1954.

H. Rider Haggard, **Eric Brighteyes**, Macdonald, 1949.

H. Treece, **Viking Trilogy** (3 vols.), Puffin, 1967.